D0101216

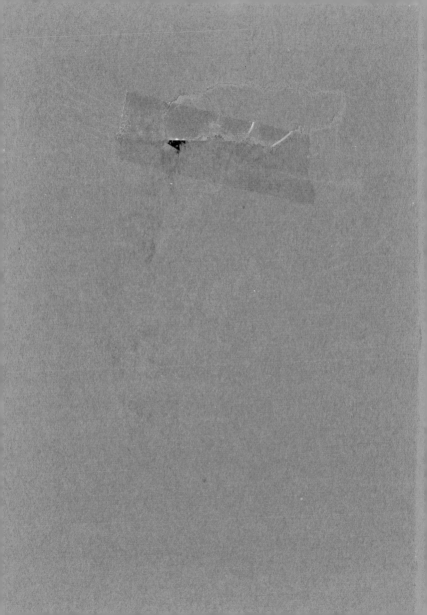

ORIEL GUIDE

ARCHITECTURE OF FRANCE

From Caves to Corbusier

THE ORIEL GUIDES

The series is edited by Bruce Allsopp, *B.Arch.*, *Dip.C.D.*, *F.R.I.B.A.*, *A.M.T.P.I.*, who is Senior Lecturer in Architecture in the University of Durham and Chairman of the Society of Architectural Historians of Great Britain. Ursula Clark is photographic editor.

ARCHITECTURE

of

FRANCE

by
BRUCE ALLSOPP
and
URSULA CLARK

ORIEL PRESS LTD

Published by
ORIEL PRESS LTD
at 27 Ridley Place, Newcastle upon Tyne
their London Office being at
2 Ellis St., Sloane St. S.W.1.
Text set by Northumberland Press Ltd
Printed in Great Britain by
Tyne Printing Works Ltd
Newcastle upon Tyne

Contents

ACKNOWLEDGEMENT

The authors gratefully acknowledge the generous
help which has been given to them by many people.
Special thanks are due to the Rector of King's College,
Newcastle upon Tyne, to the staffs of the Library, the
Printing Section and the Department of Photography
at King's College; also to Mr. David Hale for his
encouragement and good advice.

FRANCE

6

Pas-de-Calais · ARTOIS · FLANDRE · BELGIQUE · ALLEMAGNE · Nord · PICARDIE · Somme · Seine-Maritime · Oise · Aisne · Ardennes · ÎLE-DE- · Manche · Calvados · Eure · Seine-et-Oise · Marne · LORRAINE · Meuse · Moselle · Bas-Rhin · NORMANDIE · Orne · Seine-et-Marne · FRANCE · Seine-et-Marne · CHAMPAGNE · Meurthe-et-Moselle · ALSACE · Finistère · Côtes-Du-Nord · Ille-et- · Eure-et-Loir · Aube · Haute-Marne · Vosges · Ht-Rhin · BRETAGNE · Mayenne · MAINE · ORLÉANAIS · Loiret · Yonne · Hte · Saône · Belfort · Morbihan · Vilaine · Sarthe · Loir-et-Cher · Côte-D'or · Doubs · Loire-Atlantique · ANJOU · Maine-et-Loire · Indre- · TOURAINE · et-Loire · Cher · BOURGOGNE · FRANCHE-COMTÉ · Jura · SUISSE · Deux- · BERRY · NIVERNAIS · Nièvre · Vendée · POITOU · Sèvres · Vienne · Indre · Saône-et-Loire · AUNIS · Charente · BOURBONNAIS · Creuse · MARCHE · Allier · Ain · Haute-Savoie · ET-SAINTONGE · Charente · Haute-Vienne · Rhône · SAVOIE · Maritime · ANGOUMOIS · LIMOUSIN · Puy-de-Dôme · LYONNAIS · Loire · Savoie · Corrèze · AUVERGNE · Isère · Gironde · Dordogne · Cantal · Hte-Loire · DAUPHINÉ · ITALIE · GUYENNE- · Lot-et- · Lot · Ardèche · Drôme · Htes-Alpes · Garonne · Tarn-et- · Aveyron · Lozère · Basses-Alpes · ET-GASCOGNE · Garonne · LANGUEDOC · Gard · Ct venaissin · Alpes-Maritimes · Landes · Gers · Tarn · Vaucluse · Cté DE · Bouches- · PROVENCE · NICE · BÉARN · Haute- · Hérault · Du-Rhône · Var · Basses-Pyrénées · Garonne · Cté DE · Aude · ESPAGNE · Hautes-Pyrénées · Ariège · FOIX · ROUSSILLON · Pyrénées-Orientales

---

Nymphaeum, sanctuary of nymphs

Ogee, combination of convex and concave curves

Order, see p. 18

Oriel, a small room or recess with a polygonal window usually corbelled out from a wall

Pediment, a roof end enclosed by cornices in classical architecture (p.19)

Pilaster, a pillar of rectangular plan attached to a wall

Pinnacle, a slender turret or spiry structure

Quoins, corner stones

Rib, projecting structural member of a vault

Rococo, originally a term of abuse, now means lighter and more elegant development of Baroque

Romanesque, architecture developed from Roman

String Course, horizontal moulding on face of building

Tracery, patterned supports for glazing

Transept, part of a cruciform church projecting at right angles to main axis

Transom, cross bar of window

Triforium, gallery or arcade over aisle

Vault, arched covering in stone or brick

Voussoirs, truncated wedge-shaped blocks forming an arch

Glossary

Abacus, the top or bearing slab of a capital

Abutment, solid resistance to the lateral thrust of an arch

Ambulatory, walking way

Apse, semi-circular or multangular termination to a plan

Atrium, court

Barbican, outer fortification protecting bridge, entrance etc.

Baroque, rich, bold and vital architecture after the high Renaissance

Basilica, originally a hall of justice, later a type of plan (p. 20)

Buttress, structure built against wall to resist pressure

Byzantine, of Constantinople (Byzantium)

Cella, main compartment of a temple

Chancel, east end of main body of a church

Chevet, apse with ambulatory off which are chapels (p. 32)

Clerestory, windows above adjacent roof

Corbel, bracket, usually stone

Corbel vault, dome, see p. 8

Corinthian Order, p. 18

Composite Order, p. 18

Crossing, intersection of nave and transepts

Doric Order, p. 18

Flamboyant, later Gothic with flame-like tracery

Fluting, vertical channelling (on column)

Gargoyle, grotesque water spout

Groin, intersection of vaulting surfaces (without ribs)

Impost, member on which arch rests

Ionic Order, p. 18

Keystone, central stone which locks an arch

Lantern, glazed structure which rises above roofs

Lierne, short intermediate rib in vaulting

Machicolation, projection with floor opening for dropping things on enemy

THE Oriel Guide is designed to help the more discriminating visitor so that, whether he goes to remote places or pushes his way through the throng at Nôtre Dame in Paris, he may look with a discerning eye, recognize different kinds of architecture and understand something of their meaning and their beauty.

The book is arranged in three parts. Pages 8 to 17 give a very concise history of architecture which you should read first. From page 18 to page 87 French architecture is explained in chronological order from ancient times to the present day. The last four pages of this section are given to vernacular architecture, cottages, farm houses and the like. The third section, on pages 92 to 95 is devoted to touring routes. These are interesting holiday tours, quite apart from the architecture, but they are devised so that each one gives an opportunity to study a particular sort of architecture. As far as possible the less busy roads and the most interesting places have been chosen.

You can read the whole book systematically before you start, but you may still find it useful to dip into during the tour, and it has been designed for that. Each page, or pair of pages, is complete as a small subject study, and by occasional browsing you can get to know the different kinds of architecture—but do read pages 8 to 17 first.

Mannerism, critical term applied to proto-Baroque

Mansard, roof with steep lower, shallow upper slope

Misericord, hinged seat to support standing person

Module, basic measure of proportion

Narthex, arcaded entrance porch (to basilica)

POST AND LINTEL

This is the simplest and was the earliest structural form. It was the basis of Classical architecture as it evolved in ancient Greece. It persisted in Roman architecture.

ROUND ARCH AND VAULT

The Romans introduced the round arch, the barrel vault and the cross vault to western architecture. The barrel vault is like a tunnel, and difficult to light with windows in the side. The cross vault is, in effect, the intersection of two barrel vaults. Romanesque architecture was a development of the same basic structural principles.

THE CORBEL DOME

This was used in the 'bee-hive' tombs at Mycenae and later in the *trulli* of Apulia (Italy). It is also found in the *borries* and well heads of Provence. It is the basis of eastern domed architecture which, from Constantinople, influenced French Romanesque architecture, as at Le Puy and Périgueux (p. 38).

Page 8   Nîmes, Corinthian columns and
lintel of the Maison Carrée.
Autun, Roman City Gate.
Tournus, Round arches and transverse
Provence, a well head near Apt.
barrel vaults.

Page 9   Amiens, Gothic vaulting.
Fontainebleau, Façade to the Cour
de la Fontaine
Paris, Pavillon Suisse by Corbusier
in the Cité Universitaire
Paris, Pont Alexandre III

THE POINTED ARCH AND RIBBED VAULTING

These were introduced in late Romanesque architecture and made Gothic architecture possible. The distinguishing feature of Gothic architecture is *the separation of structural rib and pier from panelled infilling*. This occurs both in timber and in stone building. The idea was used long before the Middle Ages in timber building but not in stone.

THE RENAISSANCE

Up to the Renaissance (fifteenth century) the character or style of architecture changed in accord with improvements in structural techniques. With the Renaissance the supposed formal values of Classical architecture were reasserted and structural design had little effect upon the style of architecture.

INDUSTRIAL AGE

In the industrial age, the Classical ideal gave way to the need for new structural techniques, and the details of older architecture continued to be applied, but with less and less conviction.

MODERN ARCHITECTURE

Modern design is again based upon the logical use of structural forms, and mainly exploits the possibilities of much improved lintels, made of steel or concrete. Most modern architecture is thus different from post-Renaissance architecture, and has an affinity with Medieval and earlier ways of building.

Lascaux, Cave Painting

Carnac, Alignements

About fifteen to twenty thousand years ago men decorated caves to use them as places of worship. They converted these naturally enclosed volumes to make them significant in relation to their own needs and aspirations. Thus they anticipated the achievements of men in later times who built significantly and so made architecture.

France is rich in cave art especially in the Dordogne valley.

Before 1500 B.C. the peoples of France had raised colossal stones to make monumental architecture, as also did the Britons at Stonehenge on Salisbury Plain. The greatest architectural achievement of this era, in France, was the *alignements* near Carnac, on the south coast of Brittany. These are vast avenues of stones, leading to huge stone altars, and suggesting tremendous roofless cathedrals. They also made impressive tombs, in tumuli, which were the same basic idea as the pyramids of Egypt.

From the first century B.C. to about A.D. 500 Roman architecture flourished in France (Gaul) which was a highly civilized and wealthy part of the Roman Empire. Some of the finest Roman buildings which still exist are in France.

The characteristics of Roman architecture are:

   a. The 'orders' or standardized columns and capitals which the Romans learned from the Greeks.

   b. The round arch and the round vaulted forms which they themselves developed.

Nîmes, Maison Carrée

Pont du Gard

Poitiers, St.Jean   Merovingian

St.Germigny-des-Près.   Carolingian

MEROVINGIAN PERIOD *c.* 500-751. With the establishment of the barbarian Franks in Gaul by Clovis I (ruled 481-511) Roman influence in architecture remained very strong, especially in the Church. Many of the bishops were of Roman senatorial families and churches continued to be built on the basilican plan, that is, with a narthex, a wide nave, narrow aisles and an apse at the end (p. 20). After the death of Lothar I in 561 there was a long civil war and degradation of architecture.

CAROLINGIAN PERIOD 751-987. Very little survives from the eighth and ninth centuries in France. Under Charlemagne Byzantine influence from Constantinople gained strength, especially in decoration and the planning of churches.

EARLY ROMANESQUE (tenth and eleventh centuries) Until the tenth century Norman raids and invasions, reaching to the heart of France, destroyed much architecture and retarded development. From the treaty of St. Clair-sur-Epte in 911, and the creation of the Duchy of Normandy, architecture recovered. There was much rebuilding, crude at first but leading to the great age of Romanesque architecture under the Capetian dynasty in the 12th century. After 1000 A.D. men tended less to look back to Rome and gained confidence to invent and develop a new architecture.

After an age of trouble and devastation a relatively fireproof type of construction was adopted for churches and experiments were made with vaults and domes.

Romanesque architecture has strong regional characteristics.

Tournus, St.Philibert

Cluny,
Plan of the Romanesque Abbey Church

Typical Roman   Romanesque

Capital at Issoire

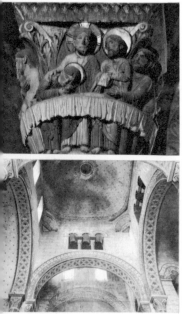

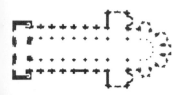

Vaults at Issoire

Plan of Issoire

FIVE aspects of Romanesque architecture are specially interesting:

a. Whereas the Romans used the column (order) as a decoration *round* their arched construction, the Romanesque builders made the column *support* the arch, and varied its proportions and design according to the load it had to carry.

b. Roman capitals had been standardized, and all alike in any one colonnade; but Romanesque architects allowed each capital to be an individual work of art, and this became a great age of sculpture.

c. The beautiful internal volumes of Romanesque architecture come from the experimental and imaginative treatment of the vaults as structural forms. (Compare with modern architecture).

d. Stone-vaulted buildings replaced timber-roofed churches. This relatively fireproof mode of construction necessitated a narrowing of the nave because it was not possible to build a vault over a very wide span at this date. The result was the characteristic long vista of the medieval church.

e. The *chevet* is the characteristic east end of a French medieval cathedral. It evolved in Romanesque architecture from the apse of the basilica, by taking the aisle round the end to give access to apsidal chapels. This was not only convenient as a way of planning: it also formed a structural system to buttress the high vaults of the church.

Le Mans Cathedral, Nave Arches

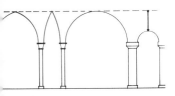

Comparison of Round
and Pointed Arches

Reims Cathedral, the Chevet

Two structural features distinguish Gothic architecture:

    a. Ribbed vaulting
    b. The pointed arch

Probably the earliest use of ribbed vaulting on a large scale was in the Romanesque cathedral of Durham in England, about 1099. This invention separated the structure into ribs and panels, into skeleton and flesh—or membrane. Gothic architecture shows a continuous refinement and expression of the structural form. It is a vertebrate architecture.

The pointed arch had an enormous advantage over round arches because, when round arches are used over varying spans, the tops of the arches come at different levels. With pointed arches, by varying the curves, the tops of the arches can be kept in line.

In France the *chevet* (see p. 44) was developed, unlike England, where the usual east end of a cathedral is square with a great window.

As vaults were made more elaborate, bigger and higher, their outward thrust had to be retained by better buttressing. Thinking in terms of skeletal lines of thrust, the Gothic architects developed the flying buttress which carries the thrust over the aisle, and by using the counterweight of pinnacles, to turn it downwards, keeps it within the piers of masonry.

Gothic architecture can be described as structural poetry. To appreciate a Gothic cathedral one should try to *feel* the structure just as, in a different way, one appreciates the structural pattern of a sonnet or a fugue in music.

Carcassonne, City Walls

Aigue Mortes, Fortifications

Josselin, Castle Walls and Towers

Rouen, Timber - Framed House

DURING the middle ages English kings fought to establish claims to large parts of France, and latterly to the crown of France (Hundred Years War 1337-78 and 1413-53). Cities were strong points and many walls, towers and gateways survive. The design of these follows European defensive techniques of the time, and the whole pattern of defence may be seen preserved, and restored, at Carcassonne. Aigues Mortes is another nearly complete example of the fortified town.

The houses of the nobility were likewise defended. Some of the best examples are along the river Dordogne where the tourist can combine them with caves and Romanesque churches. Such castles are usually placed on a naturally strong position. The round, crenellated tower came to be the most conspicuous architectural feature of French castles and was carried on into the early Renaissance châteaux, and into Scottish 'baronial' architecture which was derived from France.

The Gothic way of design was based upon logical structural techniques, so the appearance varied according to the materials used and the purpose of the building. Thus castles have a quite different character from churches, and the framed timber structure of houses is within the splendid tradition of Gothic architecture.

Gothic architecture is like modern architecture and not to be thought of just as a style. It is a complete and organic system of design.

Château de Chenonceaux

Fontainebleau, Le Breton's Work

Fontainebleau, Primaticcio's Work

Paris, Luxembourg Palace

At the end of the fifteenth century Classical architecture had been re-established in Italy, but the medieval way of building persisted in France. There seems to have been no enthusiasm, among French architects, for a change, but fashionable taste, for at least the outwardness of Latin culture, made kings and the nobility demand buildings in the Renaissance manner.

Some Italian artists came to work in France, notably Leonardo da Vinci who lived at Amboise. The Italians had to come to terms with French building methods, a different climate, the ignorance of classical detail among French craftsmen and the obstinacy of men skilled in a great, and still living, medieval tradition.

At first Classical design was incorrect and superficial but, with the work of the French architect, Le Breton, at Fontainebleau (1528-1540), a break-through was made and a truly French Renaissance way of building emerged.

This was developed by the Italians, Serlio at Ancy-le-Franc (1546) and Primaticcio at Fontainebleau (1568). In the chaotic state of France, after the death of Henry II in 1559, until the Edict of Nantes giving tolerance to Protestants in 1598, their purity of style was lost. Lescot, at the Louvre, and Philibert de l'Orme at Anet, Chenonceaux, etc., designed very freely. De l'Orme propagated revolutionary ideas in his book *L'Architecture* (1567) and invented a French 'order' with rusticated columns. This was exploited by Salomon de Brosse at the Luxembourg Palace in Paris which is the climax of the experimental stage of French Renaissance architecture.

Château de Maisons

Paris, Sorbonne Church

Versailles, Chapel

Paris, The Panthéon

THE culmination came in the work of François Mansart (1598-1666) who was probably the greatest French Renaissance architect. He created a pure Classical style which was completely French, and everything built later derives to some extent from his genius. His work seems to be founded upon that of Serlio and Primaticcio.

The French Academy for the visual arts was established in 1648, and greatly strengthened under Colbert in 1663. A French Academy was founded in Rome in 1666, the year of Mansart's death and of Wren's great opportunity after the Fire of London.

Under the Academy, and government patronage, architectural taste was organized and disciplined. A major industry, in the making of *objets d'art* and furnishings, was established, as part of a deliberate policy to make France outstanding as an artistic nation. This has proved to be of enormous economic advantage to France.

The architectural manner of F. Mansart was developed and made more grand by his sister's grandson, Jules Hardouin Mansart, who worked at Versailles and built the Dome of the Invalides in Paris.

Rococo taste had little effect on the outward appearance of French architecture, owing mainly to the discipline of the Academy. Until the Revolution in 1789 there was a gradual change towards a more severe classicism, culminating in The Panthéon in Paris (begun 1757), and this neo-classicism was taken over as the architecture of Napoleonic France after the revolutionary period.

Paris, Rue de Rivoli

Paris, Library of St. Geneviève

Paris, Gare d'Orleans

Ronchamp, Chapel of Nôtre Dame

Outline

19th and 20th Centuries

In the nineteenth century French architecture was strongly influenced by academic attitudes; but whereas correctness of Classical proportion had been of primary importance in neo-classicism of the late eighteenth century, there was a swing, in the nineteenth, towards scholarly eclecticism, i.e., the selection of decorative motifs from a wide variety of antique precedents. Students were trained to make very elaborate drawings and the realities of building for modern people were not infrequently obscured.

In planning, the *Beaux Arts* tradition was dominant and architects often treated architecture as though it were an abstract art. Symmetry was taken to such extremes as to discredit this fundamentally valuable way of design.

The Gothic revival made less headway in France than in England or America, but it produced an outstanding figure in Viollet-le-Duc (1814-79) who understood the structural quality of true Gothic design and foreshadowed some aspects of the modern movement. He influenced people towards the modern appreciation of medieval architecture and restored many cathedrals. The French were ingenious in adapting iron to design in the grand manner.

Though Perret is regarded as a pioneer of modern architecture, he is, as such, a rare figure in France where modern ideas of design had to contend against deeply entrenched academicism. The moderns have had a hard battle which has culminated in the triumphs of the French-Swiss architect, Le Corbusier. Though he himself has not had a major architectural opportunity in France, the modern idiom is now established.

Athens, The Parthenon (447–32 B.C.)

The Orders; Tuscan, Doric, Ionic, Corinthian, Composite

CLASSICAL architecture evolved in the Ægean area after the Minoan (ancient Cretan) and Helladic (Mycenæan) civilizations had perished. It was essentially an architecture of post and lintel. At first it was often in timber and forms which had been invented in the age of timber building were later (sixth century) adapted for designs in stone.

Two styles of *orders* or columns were used up to the fourth century when the Corinthian order was invented. The original orders were the Doric and Ionic.

The Romans altered the Doric order and added two more types, the Tuscan and the Composite orders. These five orders were the basic grammar of their architecture. All the parts had fixed and proper proportions. The architect was expected to design with these fixed orders—to arrange them, not to alter them, except in minor ways.

The Romans developed the use of the round arch to span bigger openings than it was practically possible to do with lintels. This was a great advance, but they seem to have thought it was necessary to enclose the arch within a framework of the orders, to make it proper architecture. The framework consisted of correct columns with their appropriate cornice. The diagram to the left shows the relationship of the old orders to the new system of construction with arches. Notice that the orders have here no structural value. This is the conservative aspect of Roman design.

Old Orders,
New Construction in Roman Architecture

Nîmes, The Maison Carrée (16 B.C.)
Puy de Dôme

THE best surviving example of a Roman temple to be found anywhere is at Nîmes, in France. Notice the very fine detail of the capitals and base mouldings. The date is 16 B.C. and the temple is typical of the best Hellenistic tradition —that is to say it shows Roman architecture which preserves the elegance and refinement of Greek design. The nature of Classical architecture is such that, though this is in fact a small building, we have only to imagine it twice the size to get a very good idea of what the major Roman temples looked like. This is because, in Classical architecture, the scale of the building is not related directly to the human figure but, in accordance with strict theoretical rules, to the height chosen for the columns.

On the summit of the Puy de Dôme (Auvergne), a volcanic mountain near Clermont-Ferrand, there are ruins of a Temple of Mercury. (There was one similarly dedicated on Montmartre in Paris.) Puy de Dôme is worth visiting for the choice of site; Nîmes for the actual architecture.

Generally Roman architecture is seen at its most conservative in temple design. The main difference from a Greek temple is that there are seldom colonnades all round the building, but in Roman Gaul the Celtic tradition of a rectangular central *cella*, with columns all round, persisted. No complete example of this type of temple survives.

Remains of the Temple of Mercury

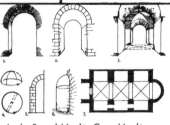

Arch, Barrel Vault, Cross Vault,
Dome, Apse, Basilican Plan

THE Romans developed vaulting—the barrel, or tunnel vault; the cross vault which is the intersection of two tunnels; and the dome which is a sort of barrel vault over a circle in plan. They could build them in brick or stone, but often they used concrete made from cement or lime.

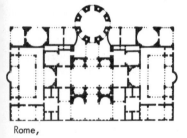

Rome,
Baths of Caracalla (A.D. 211-17)

The key to Roman planning—an aspect of architecture in which they excelled—is the roof or vault forms. The cross vault went over a square on plan, the barrel over a rectangle, and the dome over a circle. Thus it is usually possible to 'read' the ceilings from the ground-plan or ruins of a Roman building.

As you walk among Roman ruins try to keep in mind the plan shapes. You can learn to visualize the complete structure and so imagine the kind of spaces which were enclosed. It is thus possible to get a feeling of what the buildings were like, as architecture, simply by concentrating upon the form of roof which was possible and probable, and imagining oneself inside.

The Romans also used post and lintel methods of construction and could make much longer beams than the Greeks.

Pont du Gard

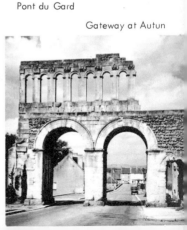

Gateway at Autun

The best example of the Roman genius in structural design is the Pont du Gard. In summer this is seen at its most majestic by swimming in the river. The best examples of Roman skill in architectural planning are outside France, in Italy and at Trier, on the German bank of the Moselle, for example.

One of the finest applications of the new system of construction, with arches, to civic design, is to be seen in the two gateways at Autun. The pictures on this page show the progressive aspect of Roman design.

Nîmes, The Amphitheatre
(Probably c.30 B.C.)

131 m. x 100 m.

21,000 seats

Used as a fortress by the Visigoths

Became slum dwellings until 19th
Century

Consider the structure as a means of
supporting ramped seating and
providing access to it.

Decorative Mosaic

Mars and Venus (2nd Cent.A.D.)
Typical of popular taste

Detail from an altar of Mithras
A superb example of Roman cult
sculpture

THE student of Roman architecture in France
should not neglect the museums, especially the
Louvre in Paris, where fine examples of the
sculpture, sculptural decoration and mosaics may
be seen. Roman civic, religious and domestic
architecture was very much embellished with
representational art which influenced both
Medieval and Renaissance art in Europe.

The Crypt at Tournus, St.Philibert. 10th Century

Top, St.Germigny-des-Prés

Middle, Tournus, the Chevet

Tournus, Plan

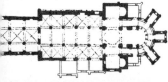

THE Roman way of building continued, under the Merovingian kings of the Franks, until the seventh century; and under the next dynasty, the Carolingians, there was little progress in architecture, though Charlemagne did encourage the influence of Byzantine ways of building. The best example is outside the modern boundaries of France at Aachen. The restored church of St. Germigny des Prés dates from 806 (see p. 11). This Byzantine type of centralized plan did not find favour in the West, but it does mark the beginning of a new and greatly creative phase in the history of architecture. From the ninth century architecture no longer looked back to Rome but, falteringly at first, and with tremendous confidence after the first millenium, it looked forward.

One may look at Romanesque architecture to see nearly all the problems of medieval cathedral planning solved in prototype, as, for example, at Tournus where all the basic concepts of cathedral design had been worked out fifty years before William the Conqueror landed in England.

Structurally, Romanesque architecture advanced from what the Romans had been able to do. In the process it had to abandon the crippling limitations of design within the orders (see p. 18). It started to grow afresh and the qualities we look for are inventiveness, enthusiasm, freshness of approach, a vital and experimental attitude to design. All these we find abundantly.

Aix-en-Provence, Baptistry (5th Cent?)

Burgundy, Vézelay
Central West,
Périgueux, St.Étienne

Auvergne,
Clermont-Ferrand, N.D.du Port
Normandy, Mont St.Michel

ROMANESQUE architecture is found throughout France but may best be seen and studied in five distinct areas:

PROVENCE, BURGUNDY, THE CENTRAL WEST, AUVERGNE, NORMANDY.

Romanesque

PROVENCE is the most Roman part of France, and being the most conservative of Roman traditions is the least adventurous in Romanesque architecture. It was also open to the Mediterranean and influences from Italy. Climatically, racially and linguistically it is distinct.

The Roman basilican form is characteristic. It is architecturally rather plain and its very simple heavy vaulting produces austere, sometimes gloomily cave-like interiors. The simple beauty of these is, in many cases, marred by nineteenth- and twentieth-century decorations of very low aesthetic value.

The unenterprising attitude to structural technique has resulted in most of the more complex Provencal churches being dark inside because of the crude vaulting and lack of clerestory lighting. Occasionally, as at St. Paul de Vence, and the chapels of Tourrettes-sur-Loup and Villefranche, there are fine examples of modern art. Generally it is massing, silhouette and the beautiful texture of stone walls that we look for.

Aix-en-Provence, the Cloister

St.Paul-de-Vence with Romanesque Church

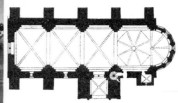

Le Thor, Plan (see p.28)

28 | Romanesque

PROVENCE

Le Thor, c. 1200 (Compare Chartres begun 1194: pages 46, 47.)

Romanesque

THE ancient kingdom of Burgundy extended north from Provence and was easily accessible up the Rhone and Saône valleys. Though important Roman remains exist (e.g. Autun) the vernacular architecture of Burgundy, with its high-pitched roofs, is akin to that of south Germany and indicates a break-away from the Roman tradition.

Burgundian Romanesque was the most adventurous and influential. This was partly due to the primacy of the Abbey of Cluny (church destroyed in 1798) which sent architects all over France, and partly to the character of the Burgundians, a people with a sense of quality in architecture as in wine and food. Thus Burgundy is a particularly pleasant holiday touring area.

Three examples illustrate distinct aspects of the Romanesque way of design: Autun, Tournus (see also p. 24) and Vézelay.

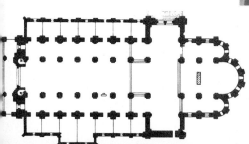

Autun, the Cathedral
(1090–1132)

Note, Basilican plan with three apses, and pointed arches in Romanesque design

Autun Cathedral (1090-1132)

Above, Tympanum signed by Giselbertus

Below, the crossing, note the pointed
barrel vaults - an old fashioned
structural design for its date. Compare
with Durham Cathedral (1093-1133)

Tournus, St.Philibert, (c.1009)

Notice, the transverse barrel vaults which permit clerestory lighting

A very austere and, in its day, very avant gard design.

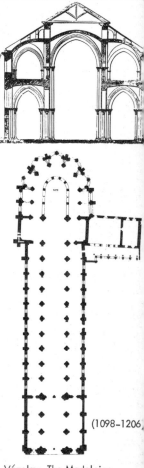

(1098–1206)

Vézelay, The Madeleine

Interior, cross section, plan
and Chapter House entrance

THE most important Romanesque architecture of this region lies in or near the Allier valley, adjoining the steep eastern side of the *Massif Central*. Auvergne was a rich Roman province which suffered terribly from plague in the sixth century. It recovered slowly, having probably lost much of the Romanized element in the population. It was resettled from other areas and from the mountain (Celtic) peoples who came into their own again. Its patois is as distinct as that of Provence and more difficult to understand.

The simple basilican plan of churches developed into the chevet, as in neighbouring Burgundy. The form of the central tower is distinct as a structural adventure. The design of columns and capitals remains remarkably true to Roman, in general forms, but the detail is rich and expressive *within* this discipline.

Building stones are dark in this volcanic region. The church of St. Austremoine at Issoire is the finest and most fully developed of the Auvergne group. Though the colour decoration (1862) has been much criticized it does give a better idea of what such churches looked like than the bare walls of most churches. Issoire is a good centre for visiting the Auvergne churches. The most remote church of Orcival is fortunate in its lovely setting and should not be missed. It has suffered least in restoration and contains a superb twelfth-century coloured statue of the Virgin and Child.

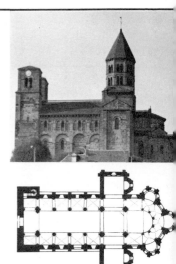

St. Nectaire

Clermont-Ferrand. N.D. du Port

Issoire, St.Austremoine

12th Century. Colour decorations restored 1862

Detail of Capital

ISSOIRE   St. Austremoine
(12th Century)

The Chevet and "shouldered" tower

Cross Section

Longitudinal Section

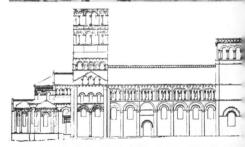

Romanesque

Souillac, Apse of the basilican Abbey Church

ONE visits the Central West for two aspects of Romanesque architecture, both rooted in the tradition of the Roman basilican plan, of which there is a superb example at Souillac.

At Périgueux the cathedral of St. Front has the same plan as St. Mark's in Venice (which was modelled upon the Church of the Holy Apostles at Constantinople). It is the main example of the Byzantine influence which spread across central France, as well as up through central Europe to Scandinavia. St. Front is a Romanesque domed church with the domes carried upon *pendentives*; i.e., segments of spheres, as at St. Sophia in Constantinople (Istanbul). St. Front has been heavily restored but the structural forms are valid and original Romanesque on a grand scale. Notice at Périgueux the extreme austerity of an architectural design which, in the Byzantine way, offered large surfaces for colour decoration. Angoulême is a more simple treatment of a basilican church roofed with domes instead of vaults.

At Poitiers the church of Nôtre Dame la Grande is an aisled basilica with a fine treatment of the vault at the crossing and vivid colour decoration which is partly original.

Souillac, sculptured portal, Isiah.

Souillac

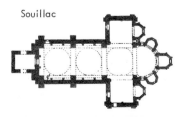

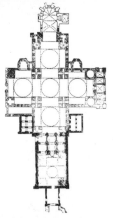

Top Left, Angoulême Cathedral (1105–30)

Right, Périgueux, St.Front (c.1120)

The central dome on pendentives
(A pendentive is the curved triangle
making the transition from a square
to a circular plan shape)

Plan of St.Front
(Based on the Church of the Holy Apostles,
Constantinople and St.Mark, Venice)

Poitiers, Nôtre Dame la Grande
(1130–45)
Detail of the West Front

Poitiers, St.Hilaire (1025–49.
Vaults 12th and 19th Cents.)

Poitiers, St.Jean (c.7th Cent.)

Mont St.Michel, the Nave

Caen, Abbaye aux Dames

THE Duchy of Normandy was the base for the conquest of England in 1066. The Normans developed a distinct version of Romanesque architecture which they had learned in France, having devastated large tracts of it before they settled and started to rebuild. Theirs is an austere and often rather crude architecture, more different from Roman than any other Romanesque—as one would expect. It is big in scale, simple in structure and coarse in detail. The best of it is in England where the Normans, having learned the art of architecture in France, had enormous opportunities which culminated in Durham, where ribbed vaulting was first used on a large scale. This was the invention which, more than the pointed arch, made Gothic architecture possible.

Late Norman Romanesque architecture shows us how the great achievement of Gothic architecture began, and Normandy was a seed ground of French Gothic architecture. We see this especially at Coutances, at Mont St. Michel, at Chartres and at Le Mans.

Mont St.Michel, Crypt

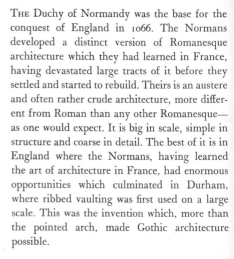

The Lantern

COUTANCES

CATHEDRAL

The Chevet

The Nave

St. Quentin

GOTHIC architecture grew out of Romanesque, within which system of design the two major elements of Gothic architecture had already been developed—the pointed arch (e.g. Autun) and the ribbed vault (e.g. Durham). But whereas Romanesque flourished most in the southern half and the west of France, Gothic developed in those lands which had been devastated by the Northmen.

Furthermore, William of Normandy having conquered England, and established there a dynasty which for a long time spoke French, and owned large tracts of France, the area of development was not confined within France but included England. Gothic architecture flourished from the Loire to the Tyne and its centre of gravity was poised about the English Channel.

The main difference between French and English Gothic cathedrals is that the English tend to be long and low, impressive in their mysterious depth of perspective; and French cathedrals, which are often built upon congested city sites, attained their majesty by building very high on a rather short plan. This French plan is much nearer to the Roman and Romanesque basilican form (pp. 20, 27, 29) than is the English plan. Another important difference is that instead of the chevet (a rounded end), English cathedrals, influenced by Celtic traditions and the rules of the Cistercian Order, often had a square end with a great eastern window.

St. Quentin, the Collegiate Church

Gothic

Noyon Cathedral

Amiens Cathedral

FRENCH cathedrals, being high and broad, demanded a greater degree of structural skill. It was in this field that the French Gothic architects excelled. Progress in design, as they understood it, consisted in raising the main vaults ever higher upon the slenderest possible pillars, thus reducing structural members to a minimum and creating vast openings which could be panelled with coloured glass. Aesthetically the French cathedral was conceived as an etherially designed enclosure of space transfused with coloured light. Through loss of the glass in many cases, and darkening where, as at Chartres, it has survived, this vision is seldom easy to apprehend now. The Sainte Chapelle in Paris is, on a small scale, the best place to experience it—out of the main tourist season for preference!

In terms of structure the vision was realized by a beautiful system of design which carried the thrust of the main vault down over the aisles by means of flying buttresses. Note that the pinnacles serve a purpose; their weight diverts the slanting thrust of the flying arches downwards, so keeping the line of thrust within the structure. (This is necessary.) The system of design is a logical answer to the problem of enclosing more space, more lightly, within the idea of the traditional Romanesque plan.

So do not think of Gothic architecture as a sudden enlightenment. The most creative phase was already over.

Amiens Cathedral

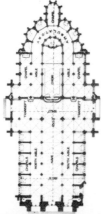

ARCHITECTURE has been called 'the art of enclosing space'. This is not completely true: architecture is more than that, but it did begin with a need for enclosed accommodation and Gothic architecture, especially, shows this aspect. Though it is often beautiful, monumental and significant from the outside, one does not *know* a Gothic church until one has been inside. (With Classical buildings the inside may be relatively unimportant.) In Gothic architecture the exterior is the expression of an enclosing structure.

St.Pol-de-Léon, Cathedral

Vitre, Timber Framed House

Tréguier, Old Houses

BRETON architecture in all periods is related to French but its special interest lies in its distinct character. It shows how architecture can express, with great sensitivity, the nature and culture of a people. Ancient Celtic traditions have been loyally preserved. The humour, individuality, hardiness and subtlety of the Bretons, combined with their skill in intricate handwork, give to Breton architecture a quaint and delightful quality. It is off the edge of cosmopolitan French culture.

APPROACHING the city you may see the mass of the cathedral. This is its only total manifestation: *stop and look.*

Proceed to the *west* end. It is the frontispiece, the overture, the preparation for entrance. The sculpture is appropriate. Look at it before you go in. It creates a mood, a suitable frame of mind.

Enter the cathedral, and if access is by a small door, off-centre (as is often the case), go at once, but slowly, to a position just inside the west door to behold the majesty of the main axis (i.e., the main vista or line of symmetry).

In a French cathedral the whole volume is visible: little is added by going down the centre of the nave. Turn right or left and go along an aisle. Here one is aware of the structure supporting the nave. If the windows are clear one sees the buttresses. The lines of them, alive with stresses of the great vault, are marked by mouldings between each window.

The aisle opens out into the transept. Pause here to appreciate the cross axis—the beam of the cross—often terminated by rose windows of great beauty. Here the eyes are naturally raised to window and vault, not lowered towards a terminal altar.

Top, Auxerre Cathedral

Middle, Chartres Entrance

Bottom, Soissons Interior

Chartres, Transepts

Beauvais, East End

The two axes cross: it is the climax of the structural design. Byzantine architects placed the face of God at this point. Renaissance architects placed a dome here, and the high altar under it when they were allowed to do so.

The choir aisle turns round the *chevet*. One feels the structure reaching over to the central climax, enfolding the altar.

Visit the side chapels and notice the screen (usually of later date) between aisle and sanctuary. The Lady Chapel is a climax in the horizontal design—the pattern of the plan—but this is an idea, not a visual architectural experience.

If possible—as it is at Reims—look back through the choir to the nave. In some cathedrals this is a superb vista ending in a western rose window.

Continue round the aisle to the other transept. The crypt is nearly always worth visiting if accessible.) Then go to a point under the crossing of the vaults, at the centre of the cross. Look into the choir and enter it, if open. Return to the crossing and feel the whole cathedral as a structure culminating above your head.

It will then be time to observe the small details, works of art and curiosities, which take their place within the tremendous architectural conception.

Don't forget to walk round outside where you will see the structural forms which make the enclosure.

Structural systems, early and late

A century of development towards
greater height and elegance of
structure

Beauvais, built 1247–1347

(Transepts 16th Century)

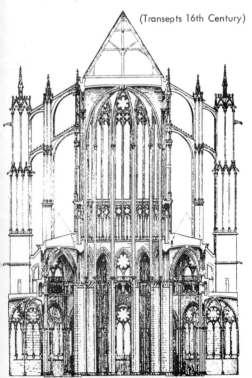

Chartres, built 1194–1260

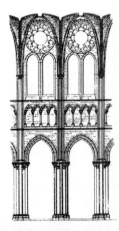

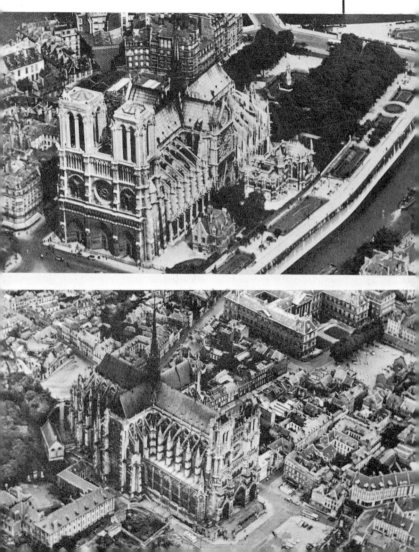

Amiens   Top Right, Chartres

Amiens

THE Gothic architect was a Master Mason, trained in the handling and working of stone. The apprentice could hope to become an architect or a sculptor. The basic craft was the same for both, and inclination or opportunity would guide towards the structural and geometric art of architecture, or the relatively personal and expressive art of sculpture. The supremacy of the sculptor in Romanesque art, making visible the scriptures to man and men to themselves, later gave place to the architect's conception of a whole building dedicated to God.

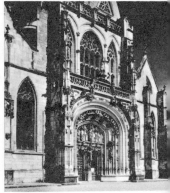

Bourg-en-Bresse, Church of Brou

Orléans, Neo-Gothic Towers
Cathedral rebuilt 17th-19th Century)

Rouen, St.Maclou

WHEN the limit of structural possibility had been reached, in the main conception, Gothic architecture became more ingenious in detail. Sometimes the cleverness is excessive and obtrusive, but much Flamboyant architecture is very beautiful. One needs to be on guard against the extreme severity of modern taste. (Flamboyant is the accepted, though rather misleading name for late Gothic architecture in France.)

Gothic

Château de Cordès

Morlaix (Brittany) Old Houses

Argentat, Houses by the Dordogne

Autun, Burgundian Houses

The Medieval Hospital at Beaune. Despite inevitable maintenance through the centuri this gives a good idea of the character of large sca medieval domestic architecture.

Top, Aigues-Mortes

Middle, Tourrettes-sur-Loup

Bottom, Walls of Avignon

EARLY Roman settlements were often in the form of fortified camps, arranged on a grid-iron plan. But in the great days of Rome cities were unfortified, and even in the troubled Merovingian period (fifth to seventh centuries) they mostly remained so. In the Middle Ages fortifications became necessary and they frequently took advantage of natural features such as cliffs. The site usually gives a clue to the design.

A typical medieval plan has four gates and main roads crossing at right angles, but the walls are roughly circular in plan, this being the shortest perimeter for defence. Towers provide strong control points and enfilade the walls. As cities grew, concentric walls were built further out, and the old walls, being demolished, often formed a ring-road. The best example is Paris where the boulevard rings followed former fortifications.

Gateways were emphasized for reasons of civic dignity but also because they had to be guarded as the obvious points of access. Battlements were, of course, functional, not decorative features. Often they were supplemented by timber staging built out from the walls, but later the battlements were corbelled with stone to provide chutes for dropping things on attackers (machicolation). A few medieval towns of military origin were set out on a grid-iron plan.

Without being actually fortified many hill towns, especially in Provence, were arranged so that the houses formed a protective ring of wall (p. 88). Such an arrangement was partly for commercial defence so that country people could be made to pay market taxes (*octroi*).

Château de Pierrefonds

Restored in the 19th Century

by Viollet-le-Duc

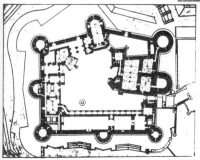

Plan of Pierrefonds showing Keep,

Court, encircling Walls and

Round Towers.

Villeneuve-lès-Avignon,
Fort St.André

The entrance is an example

of fully developed medieval

fortification.

Early Renaissance   Florence,
Pazzi Chapel (Brunelleschi)

In order to understand French architecture after 1500 it is necessary to know about the Renaissance in Italy.

Brunelleschi (1377-1446) was the first great Italian Renaissance architect. He drew inspiration from ancient Rome but felt free to modify and improve upon Roman models. Many architects followed his example and their work blends local tradition with Roman ideas. But another Florentine architect, Alberti (1404-72), wrote an influential book—*De Re Aedificatoria*—which advocated strict conformity with Roman precedents and laid down rules for design.

High Renaissance architecture followed from Alberti's teaching. His was a very limiting discipline of which Italians grew tired by the mid-sixteenth century.

The followers of Brunelleschi's way did work which was, by Alberti's standards, less pure and often much more elaborate. It led easily into the Baroque which became the general mode of design in the late sixteenth century.

Baroque architecture was partly a reaction against Alberti's formalism, partly a product of the counter-reformation, partly an expression of a society which liked ostentation and partly a development from both schools of Renaissance architecture. It is more personal and three dimensional than High Renaissance design, but retains its geometrical firmness while allowing the architect great freedom in combining the arts of painting and sculpture with architecture.

High Renaissance   Venice.
S.Giorgio Maggiore (Palladio)
Baroque   Venice,
S.Maria della Salute (Longhena)

Paris, St. Eustache   Notice pilasters between windows and on flying buttresses.

Prototype – Pavia, the Certosa

FRENCH Renaissance architecture began at the end of the fifteenth century, after Charles VIII had fought in Italy to claim the throne of Naples in 1494. Louis XII (1498-1515) also claimed Milan, and Francis I (1515-47) was defeated at the Battle of Pavia (1525). The west front of the *Certosa* (Carthusian monastery) at Pavia was started in 1491. This was especially admired and influenced French taste, as did the comfort of Italian palaces compared with French castles. New homes, mainly round Paris and in the favourite hunting country of the lower Loire, were built by kings, especially Francis I, and by the nobility. They usually had to employ French master masons who knew the old ways. These men often resisted the new fashions but were obliged to incorporate Classical details in castles which were built with many windows looking outwards. The windows remained Gothic in design and the Classical details were usually inaccurate. It was a change in fashion and not yet a different sort of architecture.

Chenonceaux

Chambord

Blois

Classical Detail on Gothic Forms

NOTICE

High pitched roofs in French Tradition (1)

Elaborate dormer windows (2)

Horizontal emphasis of string-courses and cornices (3)

Debased classical columns (4)

Elaborate sky-line (5)

Gothic Structure (6)

BEST EXAMPLES

Azay-le-Rideau (A)   Chenonceaux (B)

Chambord (C)   Blois (D)

The Cour du Cheval Blanc

The Porte Dorée

The royal palace at Fontainebleau is the key building for studying how a pure classical way of design developed in France. A French architect, Gilles Le Breton, was employed by Francis I to modernize the medieval castle in 1528. In doing so Le Breton seems to have been the inventor of a way of design which was to become the characteristic Renaissance architecture of France. He retained the high roofs and dormer windows, within the discipline of a classical form, and without that extravagance and nostalgia for Gothic decoration which we see at Chambord.

Fontainebleau, Aille de la Belle Cheminée

Ancy-le-Franc, Château by Serlio

The *Porte Dorée* was a refacing of the old medieval structure. Notice how Le Breton, the architect, made six floors of the original fit into three stories of the new classical pattern. In the north side of the *Cour du Cheval Blanc*, Le Breton was free from the old structure and this is the really important prototype.

The Italian architect, Primaticcio, imitated and perfected this new French way of design in the *Aille de la Belle Cheminée* (1568). An intermediate stage is seen in the work of another Italian, Serlio, at Ancy le Franc (1546).

FROM the fifteenth century the State was ascendant; architecture reflected this fact and there was only slow development in church design. All over France there are examples of reluctant adaptation towards the Classical idiom but, until the end of the sixteenth century, churches were being built which, apart from the trimmings, were essentially Gothic in design. These should not be lightly despised. The new movement was secular and humanistic. Church architecture was understandably out of line with the new fashions, but if one can accept the idea that old-fashioned architecture is not necessarily bad architecture, there is beauty to be found in churches of the sixteenth century. Much of it is in additions and alterations, but two great churches were built in Paris, St. Etienne du Mont (1517-1620) and St. Eustache (1532-89; west front 1772).

The interesting thing to notice, in both these, is the contrast between the majestic and strenuous structural geometry of the main conception and the superficiality of the classically inspired detail. These are still essentially Gothic buildings. The interior of St. Eustache is finer, in its austere beauty, than many medieval cathedrals. At St. Etienne one can trace the growing power of Renaissance influence as one moves from the east to the west end. The west front demonstrates the impossibility of compromise between the two great traditions of design, the Gothic and the Classical. It is interesting to compare it with the adjoining neo-classical Panthéon. Visit St. Etienne first.

Paris, St.Eustache
Interior and Plan

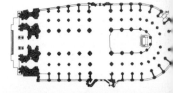

Early Renaissance

ONE of the great names in the history of Architecture is that of Philibert de l'Orme though no complete building by him survives. He wrote a book called *L'Architecture* (1567) which was an original contribution to the theory of architecture and a break with the Italian way of Renaissance design. He wrote: 'It would be much better, in my opinion, for an architect to fail in the . . . proportion and treatment of façades . . . than that he should desert Nature's excellent rules which concern the comfort, convenience and advantage of the inhabitants.' He devised a French order of architecture which was suitable for French building stones and used it in the Tuilleries Palace, of which one bay still exists in the Tuilleries Gardens, Paris.

Paris, St.Etienne du Mont, screen by P.de l'Orme
Below; a bay of the Tuilleries Palace

Chenonceaux, the Bridge Gallery

Paris, the Pont Neuf

Rennes, The Palais de Justice

(attributed to S. de Brosse)

AFTER the death of Henry II in 1559 France went through a wretched period of misgovernment and war which was unpropitious for architecture. Order was restored under Henry IV (1589-1610) who replanned Paris and built the Pont Neuf and Place des Vosges. The great architect of his day was the Huguenot, Salomon de Brosse, who built the Luxembourg Palace in Paris for Henry's widow, Marie de Medici. The plan, with its courtyard screened from the street, is typical of the great town house in France and is one of the best and most accessible examples. The Rubens paintings in the Medici Gallery of the Louvre were made for the Luxembourg Palace.

Paris, the Luxembourg Palace

Entrance Pavilion
and Screen

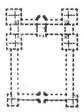

Plan

FRANÇOIS MANSART

It sometimes happens that a whole tradition culminates in the work of a single artist. This is true of the French Renaissance and François Mansart—not to be confused with J. H. Mansart, his sister's grandson (see pp. 73-75).

The two buildings which best show Mansart's genius are: the Orléans Wing at Blois and the Château of Maisons, near Paris. We look for the Classical qualities of order and restraint. His work is grand without being pompous, correct without being academic, formal without being dull. In Mansart the style imported from Italy is completely transmuted into a new architecture which is both completely French and completely Classical.

François Mansart was probably the greatest French architect since the Middle Ages and his work should be looked at with appropriate reverence. Note that he died in the year Sir Christopher Wren began to be an architect on a big scale after the Fire of London, 1666.

Blois, the Staircase

Château de Maisons

Garden Front

Plan

Detail of Entrance Front

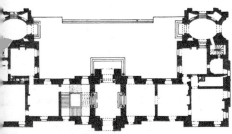

FRANÇOIS MANSART

Blois, The Orléans Wing by Mansart
The Great Staircase

LOOKING at the Orléans building we have the great staircase, built 1515-24 for Francis I, on our right. Still basically Gothic in conception it has very crude Classical detail imposed upon it. The lines of Classical design clash with the soaring structure and ascending spiral of the Gothic functional and structural conception. In 1635-38 Mansart had abandoned the idea of structural expression. The main lines are parallel to the earth. This horizontal composition is punctuated by vertical columns and window openings.

THE Château of Vaux le Vicomte (S. et M.) was designed by Louis Le Vau and completed in 1661. It is an early example of a kind of planning which is a specially French contribution to architecture.

Earlier houses and palaces had been very crudely arranged inside. At Vaux le Vicomte the interior is architecturally designed and the relationship of one room to another is carefully considered. The Vestibule and the Grand Salon form a splendid reception suite such as we now find in important embassies almost everywhere. Notice how the external elevations express the plan forms. This became an essential characteristic of architecture as taught in the French schools.

The Château of Vaux-le-Vicomte

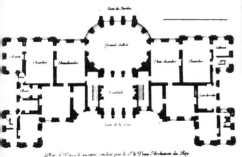

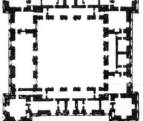

Compare with earlier planning at Ancy-le-Franc →

Lescot's work to left of tower

THE Louvre is not only a great museum and art gallery; it also exemplifies a long period of French architecture and is the key to the planning of the Champs Elysées.

The original palace, on the Isle de la Cité, began to be replaced in the sixteenth century by a palace on the right bank. This was extended along the river-side by successive monarchs as the city of Paris grew. The result was that the kings preserved, for their home, a direct way out to the country. This idea is retained in the great avenue of the Champs Elysées which is an extension of the axis of the original courtyard of the Louvre.

To follow the sequence of design first enter the Cour Carrée. The west side is the earliest. The façade to the left of the clock tower, as you stand facing towards the Champs Elysées, is by Pierre Lescot. It was built from 1546 to 1578. Half the adjoining façade of the south side is also by Lescot (1578-96). The clock tower is by Lemercier who made his design harmonize with Lescot's, and actually repeated the original design on the right-hand side of the new clock tower. His work was from 1624 to 1654. Lemercier also started the north side but this he did in the much more severe Classical style of his own day. The Cour Carrée was completed by Le Vau between 1650 and 1664.

Clock tower and to the right of it by Lemercier

North side of the Cour Carrée

The next stage can be seen in the *external* façades facing the North, East and South. The east façade is the best. It is usually attributed to Perrault but was really the work of a committee which devised a compromise scheme after a great deal of disputation. It was built between 1667 and 1674 and it is a good example of architecture which is entirely devoid of the personal qualities of a designer. It is the kind of academic Classical architecture against which the romantics revolted.

East Front of the Louvre

Louvre and Tuilleries in 1735

The Queen's Staircase,
Notice perspective painting

LOUIS XIV reigned from six years before the death of Charles I in England to the beginning of the reign of George I. While other European countries were distracted by internal divisions France attained a state of unity and efficiency in government which made her pre-eminent. French society gave the tone of good manners to Europe and led its fashions. This was the golden age of French Renaissance architecture. Under Louis XIV's ministers, and especially under Colbert, from 1661 to 1683, the State intervened in the world of art to foster brilliant results. Architecture became a deliberate expression of a splendid and pompous society.

In art, the age was characterized less by new ideas than by the exploitation and co-ordination of what had already been achieved. State patronage, on a vast scale, came just at the time when a truly French version of the Renaissance way of design had been fully developed.

The Palace and part of the Gardens

The Second Church of the Invalides
Architect, J.H.Mansart

Building started in 1692.

Compare with St.Paul's, London

THE Palace of Versailles was not a home; it was administrative H.Q. of the monarch who said 'I am the State.' It was a government building accommodating about 5,000 residents and 20,000 visiting courtiers. For anyone who is not specially interested in the background of French history Versailles can be dull.

In general the buildings at Versailles reflect the strict etiquette of court life.

Like the Louvre and Fontainebleau, Versailles began with a small house and so has no adequate architectural climax. Louis XIII built the original château which was remodelled round the Cour du Marbre. From this, wings were extended until there was sufficient accommodation for Louis XIV's court. The Palace therefore lacks that quality of unity and sense of composition which one expects in a great Classical building.

The architects of Versailles, under Louis XIV, were Le Vau and J. H. Mansart, but the painter Le Brun occupied a position as supreme artistic co-ordinator. The interiors were intended to exemplify all that was best and most costly in the arts. They are notably extravagant but, as one might expect, there is little that is artistically better than mediocre. Thus one may be well advised to go for the general impression.

Top, Cour du Marbre
Middle, Centre of the Garden Front
Bottom, Salon de l'Oeil de Boeuf

THE Chapel is, however, a splendid example of Baroque tempered by French academic Classicism, and the restored Opera House is a rich and elegant design by J. A. Gabriel, built 1753-1770.

Externally the Chapel, by J. H. Mansart, is outstanding. It is one of his best works and sets the course of sumptuous Classicism, foreshadowed in Lescot's Louvre, which culminated in the Paris Opera House (1857) and strongly influenced early twentieth-century architecture in England (e.g., Blomfield's Regent Street, London). Versailles has interest as the inspiration of much pre-modern architecture in Britain and America.

Though the façades by Le Vau and Mansart fail to be part of a unified composition, and are dull from a distance, they are splendid in themselves and should be seen from not more than 70 to 80 yards away to appreciate their fine proportions and detailing.

The gardens were originally designed by André le Nôtre on a vast scale. They were conceived as the parade ground of court life, and an effort of imagination is needed to visualize them peopled with men and women dressed like gorgeous butterflies, but living rather like ants. André le Nôtre's influence has been worldwide, not only upon park design, but upon city planning. While Paris was still a tortuous city, the avenues and crossing axes of Versailles foreshadowed the replanning of Paris by Haussmann and the lay-out of Washington likewise.

The Chapel (1696–1710) and
one of the Ailles Gabriel (1770)

Detail of the Garden Front
by J.H.Mansart 1696–85

The Petit Trianon by J.A.Gabriel 1762–8

UNDER royal patronage and a strongly established Academy, Rococo architecture did not flourish in France. The Austrian Empire enjoyed its whimsical elegancies, and England experimented with exotic styles and romantic Gothic, but French architecture became externally more severely Classical, as we see in the Ailles Gabriel at Versailles. Internally it became almost neurotically fanciful under Louis XV and elegantly severe under Louis XVI.

From the immensity of the Palace of Versailles royalty escaped to the Trianons in the park. First was the Grand Trianon, a single-story villa by J. H. Mansart; then the Petit Trianon, a Palladian type villa by J. A. Gabriel. It is his finest work.

Grand Trianon from the Peristyle

(J.H.Mansart & Robt.de Cotte)

NORTH-EAST of the Petit Trianon, across an English garden which contrasts with the formality of French landscaping but is undistinguished by English standards, lies *The Hamlet*. This is a pathetic and beautiful toy of great social and psychological interest. Architecturally it shows an awakening to the beauty of vernacular architecture long before the equivalent and more influential movement in England. Innumerable small houses emulate this precedent, set by a queen who was bored by formality, but very few capture its delightful rococo quality. The landscaping has now reached maturity. It is more beautiful than when Marie Antoinette knew it.

THE Palace of Compiègne, built by J. A. Gabriel between 1752 and 1770, 'achieves an effect at once tranquil and monumental'. Academic influence favoured such an effect. From about 1750 architects became more and more interested in archæological correctness and in a kind of planning which was almost an abstract art. In the years before the Revolution of 1789, and still more so in the troubled years after that cataclysm, architects indulged in grand architectural dreams of vast monumentality. These are recorded in elaborate and beautiful drawings, some of which may be seen in the *Concours d'Architecture*.

Real building reflects this dreaming and two big churches in Paris are academic visions come true, though on a very small scale compared with the fabulous designs submitted for the *Prix de Rome*. They are the Panthéon and the Madeleine.

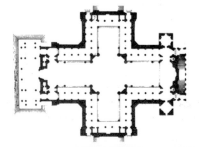

Above, The Palace of Compiègne (1752–72)
by J.A.Gabriel

Below, Paris, Plan and Interior of the
Panthéon (begun 1757)
by G.Sufflot

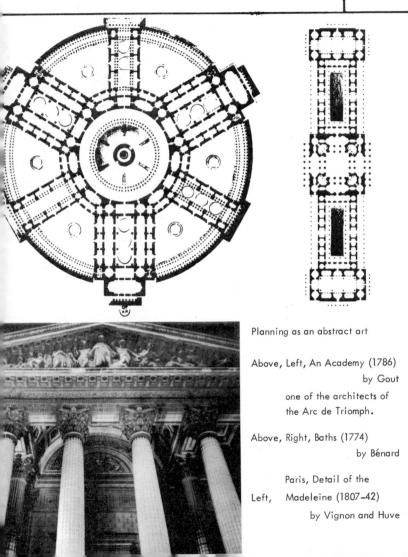

Planning as an abstract art

Above, Left, An Academy (1786)
by Gout
one of the architects of
the Arc de Triomph.

Above, Right, Baths (1774)
by Bénard

Paris, Detail of the
Left, Madeleine (1807–42)
by Vignon and Huve

THE huge Arc de Triomphe (architect Chalgrin and others) was built between 1806 and 1836. It commemorates the victories of the Grande Armée and signifies the end of an epoch in architecture. The academic regime had kept French architecture firmly in the tradition of Rome but it could not for ever hold back the tide of eclecticism, the almost universal craving for an alternative to the stale pomp of Classical design. Most people thought of turning to other old styles: very few, in the first half of the nineteenth century, could imagine a new architecture though it was already coming into being in structures made of iron.

As architects broke free from the restraint of Classical discipline, they were able to indulge that love for rich decoration which has flowered many times in the architecture of France since the fall of Rome.

In massing and planning French architecture remained largely Classical and, where possible, monumental. The special interest is in lush decoration and the use of many rich materials. The Opera House in Paris embodies the best of the French achievement in the mid-nineteenth century, and sets a standard by which to judge other works.

Above, Paris, the Arc de Triomphe

Below, Paris, St.Augustin (1860–71)

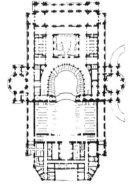

Paris, The Opera House (1860) by Charles Garnier

THE second half of the nineteenth century produced a great deal of elaborate architecture. In theory, sculptor, painter and architect, trained in the same schools, and sharing the same ideals, were working in harmony to produce splendid buildings. In fact the truly creative artists of the age worked without patronage, public understanding or sympathy. For the painter it was possible to live the life of half-starved bohemianism and still create, but the architect must have money spent on his buildings. Successful architects catered for the taste of patrons whose culture was pretentious and sometimes spurious. Their buildings often combine panache with plain vulgarity, but planning is lavish and imaginative; silhouettes are interesting and there is a comfortable generosity about much of this architecture.

Paris, Place Henri Bergson and St. Augustin

Monte Carlo, Detail of the Casino
by Charles Garnier

Calais, the Town Hall

Paris, The Eiffel Tower

Paris, Les Halles (Central Markets)

THE development of railways provided opportunities for building in iron and steel. Many of the less pretentious railway stations are worth looking at as architecture. On the model of the Gare de l'Est, Baltard, who was also architect of St. Augustin (p. 80) designed Les Halles, the Paris markets, with iron and glass roofs. The Eiffel tower, 984 feet high, was an exhibition piece and the highest building in the world in 1889 when it was built. Though reputed to be a masterpiece of lightness and strength it is in fact a crude piece of structural design by modern standards. (This could not be justly said of Beauvais Cathedral.)

Paris, Grandiose Architecture of 1900

The Petit Palais

The Grand Palais

Architect Charles Girault

Le Harvre,

(Rebuilt under the direction of Auguste Perret)

Rouen, Riverside houses from the new bridge

THE quality of French culture was such that academic influence remained strong. Ingrained habits of taste, and the tendency of an educated people to have decided views about what was good and bad in art, made the progress of modern architecture slow. Until the 1940s opportunity was mainly limited to utilitarian structures such as low-cost housing. There has been little expensive modern architecture.

The work of Perret shows progress in concrete techniques but most of his building is basically Classical and his latest manner was monumental (p. 85).

The outstanding genius has been Le Corbusier, who made architectural history with small houses that some architects would have scorned. His architecture is always creative, thoughtful, closely related to the abstractist wing of modern art and yet austerely poetic. He has created many of the prototypes of the modern international idiom and gone on to explore and create afresh, so compare his later buildings with Romanesque and remember that most of them have had to be done quite cheaply. His influence is now to be seen everywhere.

Paris, Pavillon Suisse

Marseilles, Unité d'Habitation

Marseilles, Detail of the Unité d'Habitation (1946–52)

by Le Corbusier

FAMOUS buildings like Nôtre Dame and the Louvre in Paris are to be found in any history of architecture, but most buildings are much more simple. They are what is called *vernacular architecture*, and they are often interesting and sometimes very beautiful.

Vernacular architecture derives its character from the cultural and racial history of a district, and from the climate and the natural building materials available. No complete history of vernacular architecture has yet been written so the tourist may, if he wishes, make his own original study.

How does he set about it? He chooses, or accidentally finds, a district where there is a distinct character in the cottages, farms and town houses. He thinks first about the climate and then about the local materials. How have they affected design? He then enquires about the racial history of the region. Did it remain Romano-Gallic in the Dark Ages? Was it conquered by Burgundians whose architecture resembles that of the upper Rhineland? Was there a strong Celtic tradition, as in Brittany, where cottages are like those in Cornwall or Western Ireland? Did some seventeenth-century landowner rebuild according to Renaissance principles and alter the vernacular of the whole district by his example?

Farm in Provence

Corros

Farm in Provence

Vernacular Architecture

CLIMB over the top of a pass and you may find the architecture quite different. Vernacular styles are localized and changes are abrupt. Your study may be no more than an interesting collection of photographs, or, if you stay in a district for some time you may do some genuine research. If you do, Oriel Press would be glad to hear about it.

In Provence Roman tradition remained very strong and vernacular architecture so closely resembles Roman that it is almost impossible, on stylistic evidence alone, to say when things were built. In country districts one may actually see what Roman rural architecture looked like.

Provençal Farms like Roman Villas

In Burgundy, where the rainfall is greater and there is plenty of timber on the hill-sides, the barbarian invaders established themselves and set up an important kingdom. Burgundian houses have high-pitched roofs and Roman tiles are seldom used. Many houses are timber framed and even if they are not they have the high proportions which come easily in timber building. Timber construction poses problems in foundations. The area in contact with the ground, and liable to rot, may wisely be kept small.

Burgundy looks towards the North and readily acepted ideas from Gothic design in the Middle Ages, but it is also racially different from the North, and near to influences from the conservative South, which thought of itself as upholding the values of ancient Rome. In Burgundy we find change in the vernacular but conservatism in public buildings such as churches.

Burgundian Farm

A Precinct in Bar-sur-Loup (Near Grasse)

Vernacular Architecture

ONE of the most interesting aspects of vernacular architecture in France is the way in which the Renaissance style of design, which was, as we have seen, pioneered by Le Breton (p. 62), became a vernacular. French towns owe much of their beauty and charm to the fact that this unostentatious vernacular is so common that we take it for granted. The nineteenth and twentieth centuries have produced many self-conscious designs for minor buildings which stick out as errors of taste, but in the rebuilding of devastated cities the French have evolved a new vernacular which is distinctly modern. It is a civilized urban way of design which makes unimportant buildings a discrete and pleasant foil for the many gems of major architectural achievement which abound in France and make it such a delightful place for the tourist.

Top, Paris, Ile St.Louis

Below, Rouen

Right, Paris, Ile de la Cité

These tours select the best within a convenient itinerary. Each is specialized. Tours may be combined; e.g. Roman and Romanesque. Cross references are bracketed in italics, thus: (*Roman*).

ROMAN (Can be combined with a holiday on the Côte d'Azur)
Coming from North start at AUTUN (*Romanesque*) Roman *Augustodunum*, important city on route from Boulogne (and Britain) to Lyons and South. Enter by N.80. See the Roman Porte d'Arroux (p.21). Approaching city centre turn left up the Rue de la Croix Blanche to Porte St. André which is one of the best Roman gateways in existence. Turn right and follow medieval walls to theatre which seated 18,000 people.
AUTUN to CLERMONT-FERRAND via MOULINS. (St. Pourcin is convenient staying place with good food and wine.)
CLERMONT–FERRAND, *Augustonemetum*, capital of the great Roman province of Auvergne and home of Sidonius Apollinaris (5th. Cent.) has no notable Roman remains but ROYAT, the modern spa, was founded by the Romans and on top of Puy de Dôme (accessible by car, 12 Kms.) are foundations of a great temple of Mercury Arvernorix (p.19) and one of the finest views in France.
CLERMONT to ISSOIRE (*Romanesque*) BRIOUDE (*Romanesque*) LE PUY (*Romanesque*) VALS-les-BAINS, AUBENAS. Turn right N.579 to D.I. to VALLON PONT D'ARC (Natural arch over river; worth seeing) D.4 to ST. REMÈZE, D. 201 (Cavern de Marzal worth seeing – dolmens, strange country of the Bois des Géantes). Join N. 86 to PONT ST. ESPRIT, N. 86 to PONT DU GARD, (Roman aqueduct) and NÎMES.
NÎMES, Roman *Nemausus*, the Maison Carrée (pp. 10,19) the most perfect Roman temple existing. Arena (21,000 seats) still in use (p.22) Roman arches in Jardin de la Fontaine, ' Temple of Diana,' (probably *nymphaeum*) and other Roman monuments. D. 42 to ST. GILLES (*Romanesque*); N. 572 to ARLES, probably a Greek city and Roman bridge over the Rhône on the direct route to Spain. See the Arena (21,000 seats) one of the oldest, (c.46 B.C.?) ruins of theatre, remains of Thermae (1st Cent. B.C.) and do not miss the Musée d'Art Paien.
D. 17, via FONTVIELLE (Daudet's mill) and D. 5 to ST. RÉMY; see Roman Mausoleum and Arch. Thence to AVIGNON (*Gothic Bridge*, *Palace*) and ORANGE, Roman *Arausio*, scene of disastrous defeat in 105 B.C. See, Theatre (best in Europe) and Triumphal Arch (49 B.C.) Tour may be extended to VAISON LA ROMAINE and return North through mountains via GAP and GRENOBLE.

ROMANESQUE
BURGUNDY
Start at AUXERRE (Medieval cathedral with Romanesque crypt) via N.77 to CLAMECY and N.151 to VÉZELAY. See the Basilica of St. Madeleine (c. 1150) restored by Viollet-le-Duc; very pure Romanesque interior; note Chapter House entrance similar to Kirkstall, (Leeds, England) sculptured tympanum. (Vézelay is a good staying place)

N.458 to BAZOCHES (Château) D 42 to LORMES, D.6 and N.77 to SAULIEU (famous for food) See Basilica of St. Andoche (1119), very fine sculptured capitals.

N. 80 to AUTUN (*Roman*) See cathedral: sculpture by Giselbertus. N.78 and N.481 to Sercy and after 2, kms. D.215 to TOURNUS (Alternative route via Chalons and N.6; very heavy traffic).

TOURNUS, see church of St. Philibert, very early and structurally most interesting. (pp. 8, 31). Note the nave vaults and do not miss the crypt (10th. Cent.) See the chevet from outside. D.14, D.187 and D.15 to CLUNY, see remains of greatest Romanesque abbey (pulled down 1798) N.80 and turn right along N.79 to PARAY LE MONIAL. See Basilica of Sacré Coeur (1109) modelled on Cluny.

AUVERGNE

From PARAY LE MONIAL go direct via VICHY (detour to CHATEL MONTAGNE, 12th. Cent. church.) to CLERMONT-FERRAND (*Roman*) See N.D. du Port, (11th. and 12th. Cents.) Note chevet (p.34) and south door. (Gothic cathedral) N.141A (detour to summit of Puy de Dôme well worth while) and D.216, D.27 to ORCIVAL. See church, 12th. Cent. and statue of Madonna. (Chateau de Cordès, p. 53).

D.27 and N. 683 to LE MONT DORE (Spa, winter sports.) N.496 to ST. NECTAIRE; see church, (12th. Cent.) sculptured capitals (p.34) N.496 to ISSOIRE; see church of St. Austremoine, largest of the Auvergne group, (pp.35, 36) sculptured capitals, colour decorations. (Good staying place, Detours to ST. SATURNIN, BRIOUDE and LE PUY which have important Romanesque churches. Le Puy notable for Byzantine influence).

CENTRAL WEST

From ISSOIRE westwards via N.496, D.26 and N.678 to BESSE EN CHAND-ESSE (Fortified city, Romanesque church) N.678 D.30E and D.22 to BORT LES ORGUES (14th. Cent. Château; basalt cliffs) Follow Dordogne Valley to ARGENTAT (picturesque houses, p. 53) and D. 12 to BEAULIEU (Romanesque abbey). Take left bank of the river N.140 and D.43, via LA CAVE (Caverns worth visiting, detour to PADIRAC, most spectacular of French caverns) to SOUILLAC (Abbey, sculpture, p.38) N. 703 and N. 704 to SARLAT (old houses; detour to DOMME, a Bastide, i.e. medieval military town and to medieval castle at BEYNAC which is good staying place) N. 704 to MONTIGNAC (for LASCAUX caves, p.10). N.706 to LES EYZIES (prehistory museum etc.) or N. 710 to PÉRIGUEUX; see St. Front (p. 38) St. Étienne and Roman Tour de Vésone. N. 139 to BRANT-ÔME (Medieval abbey, very photogenic) and ANGOULÊME, see the cathedral (p.38) N. 10 to POITIERS (detour via N. 139 and D.121 to AULNAY, Romanesque church and sculpture.) At POITIERS see N.D. la Grande (p.39) St. Hillaire (p.39) and St. Jean (pp. 11, 39) N.10 to DANGÉ; D.58 and D.31 to LOCHES; see St. Ours which has unique pyramidal vaults. N.143 to TOURS (Medieval cathedral). Detour for the Loire Châteaux; BEAUGENCY is a good centre).

From ORLÉANS, N.20 and N.154 to CHARTRES (pp. 46, 47, 48, 50) (rebuilt 1194-1260) Towered transepts – the original plan envisaged a nine towered cathedral.   Outstandingly important sculpture and stained glass. (There is a good train service to PARIS for St. Denis and Nôtre Dame.)

From CHARTRES, N.154 to EVREUX (early 12th. to 17th. Cent.) Old glass. A beautiful plan. N. 154 to ROUEN (pp. 52, 85) begun 1202 but notable for late Gothic tracery and beautiful towers.   See also St. Ouen and St. Maclou. N.30 and N.31 to BEAUVAIS (Detour 9 kms. from N.31 to St. Germer-de-Fly for exceptionally fine Romanesque abbey.)

BEAUVAIS (pp. 47, 48) (1247-1568) the ultimate in Gothic structural design.   After collapse in 1284 the choir vault was rebuilt, with additional piers (1337-47). N. 31 to Clermont (14th. Cent. Hôtel de Ville, restored) N.16 to Creil, N.330 to SENLIS (1153-1240, reconstructed 1504).

N. 324 to Chantilly (Château, Park).   N.16 to St. Denis.   Founded as an abbey by King Dagobert, became a national shrine and the burial place of the kings and queens of France.   Rebuilt 1136-47 with many later alterations.   Thence to the centre of PARIS for Nôtre Dame (p.49) (1163-1250 with later alterations).   A sombre but splendid and strong design characteristic of early Gothic.

RENAISSANCE AND CLASSICAL

This tour is based on Paris in the form of listed groups of buildings which may conveniently be visited in or from the capital.

GROUP I, THE LOIRE CHÂTEAUX (p. 61)

AZAY-LE-RIDEAU (1518-29); CHENONCEAUX (1513-21; bridge gallery by de l'Orme 1557); CHAMBORD (1519-44); BLOIS (13th. Cent. to 1640); CHEVERNY (1634) the typical seigneurial mansion of the 17th. Cent.

GROUP 2, FONTAINEBLEAU (pp. 62, 63) provides a conspectus of French Renaissance architecture but is specially notable for Le Breton's work (1528-46) and the Italian influence in Primaticcio's

After Fontainebleau visit ANCY LE FRANC by Serlio (pp. 63, 69,) and VAUX-LE-VICOMTE by Le Vau, Le Brun and gardens by Le Nôtre. Gardens are open Palm Sunday to November 11th. on *Saturdays, Sundays and festival days only* from 11 to 18 hrs.   Admission to the house only by permission sought in writing seven days in advance and only in the afternoons of week-days, June to October.

GROUP 3, ANET, the chapel and gateway are by de l'Orme.

ST. GERMAIN EN LAYE, a medieval castle rebuilt by Francis I.

MAISONS-LAFITTE (1642-46) one of François Mansart's finest works.

VERSAILLES—mainly for the work of J. H. Mansart and J. A. Gabriel.

GROUP 4, PARIS CHURCHES 16th. to 19th. Centuries.

ST. EUSTACHE (begun 1532); ST. ÉTIENNE DU MONT (begun 1517); CHURCH OF THE SORBONNE by Lemercier (begun 1635); THE VAL DE GRACE by F. Mansart and Lemercier (begun 1645); THE DOME OF THE INVALIDES by J. H. Mansart, (begun 1692); THE PANTHÉON by Soufflot (begun 1758); THE MADELEINE by Vignon and Huve (begun 1807); ST. AUGUSTIN by Baltard (begun 1860).

GROUP 5,   THE LOUVRE and the LUXEMBOURG PALACES.

NORMANDY
From TOURS by N. 158 to LE MANS; see Romanesque and Gothic cathedral
(p. 13), very early glass. N. 138 to ALENCON and SÉES (Gothic cathedral).
N.158 to CAEN; see Abbaye aux Hommes, Abbaye aux Dames (p. 40).
N. 13 to BAYEUX; see cathedral and the Bayeux Tapestry which is in a
house facing the south aisle. N.172 to COUTANCES (p. 41) See the
cathedral. (Detour to COUTAINVILLE for bathing, good food). N.171 to
GRANVILLE, N.173 to AVRANCHES, N.798 and D.43, D.275 to MONT
ST. MICHEL (p.40) Tour may be extended into BRITTANY or to CHART-
RES and the best of the medieval cathedrals.

GOTHIC CATHEDRALS

A round tour including most of the best. Capital letters are used for the
Gothic cathedral cities only.
Start at AMIENS (1220-88) (pp. 44, 49, 50) the 'perfect type' of French
Gothic cathedral. Begun with the nave, architect Robt. de Luzarches.
Choir and transepts by T. and R. de Cormont, father and son. Notice
specially the external stone sculpture and internal wood sculpture. N.334
to NOYON (1145-1228) (p.43) (City of St. Eloi.) N.334 and N.37 to
SOISSONS (p.46) (1180-1225) (Ancient capital of the Franks.) Apsidal S.
transept. Example of fully developed Gothic. N.2 to LAON (1160-1225)
Not strictly a cathedral, i.e. seat of a bishop, since 1789. Flat, 'English
type' east end. West front is outstanding as a design and as prototype
for Reims and other cathedrals. N.44 to REIMS (pp.13, 51) (1211-90)
Planned as the coronation church of the kings of France, hence its unusual
spaciousness at the east end with double choir aisles linked to the transepts.
The western facade was designed by Bernard of Soissons and built c. 1255-
1290. The cathedral was gutted in the first world war and has been
restored. The brilliance of the modern glass gives an idea of what medieval
glass looked like when it was new but some enthusiasts for the antique do
not admit this.
N. 51 via Epernay to Nogent N. 439 to SENS. Started about 1140 this is
the earliest of the great Gothic cathedrals. The architect, William of
Sens, is associated with the building of Canterbury. See 12th. cent. glass
in N. choir aisle. The treasure is notable. N.5 to St. Florentin (interesting church) N. 77 to AUXERRE (c. 1215-1560) mainly late Gothic of very
sensitive design. (p.46). Auxerre is the starting point of the Romanesque
tour.
From AUXERRE, N.77 to Clamecy, D.33 and N.151 to BOURGES (1192-
1275) Extreme development of the French type of plan, no transepts.
Double flying buttresses over aisles which are unique in France and resemble
Milan. 13th. Cent. glass. Return along N.151 and branch left on N.455 to
Sancerre (wine and cheese) then follow the Loire by N.751 to Sully-sur-
Loire. (Château) Cross river by N.448. Follow river by D.60 to St.
Bénoit-sur-Loire (Romanesque church) St. Germigny des Prés (p.11)
and Châteauneuf-sur-Loire. N.152 to ORLÉANS (p.52) The 13th. Cent.
cathedral was gutted in the wars of religion (1567) Restoration was started
by Henry IV in the Gothic style.